30 Days to De-Stress Your Stressful Life

by

Joyce Good Henderson

Faith's Loom Books

Contents

Chapter 1

30 Days to De-Stress Your Stressful Life

At some time in life, almost everyone notices the effects of stress in their lives, careers and relationships. Stress is actually a normal part of daily life, that helps you to seek solutions to problems, re-directs your thinking, and enables you to face life's demands with an open, flexible, and, often, positive attitude.

Any situation can cause stress, including problems with interpersonal relationships, raising children, paying bills, divorce, keeping up with a demanding daily routine, illness or death of a loved one, caring for aging parents, moving to a new house, starting or stopping a job, losing a pet, financial problems, health concerns, having a baby, unexpected changes, conflict or even a welcomed experience, such as a vacation.

Stress is the automatic, physiological effect your body experiences in any situation evoking a physical, emotional or psychological response that mobilizes you for quick action. Think fight-or-flight, or the sudden attack of a mastodon. Your body was created to handle emergencies. Unfortunately, our stress today can arise from a one-time event, as well as from a chronic, long-term onslaught.

For most of us, stress begins first thing in the morning. You awake a few minutes late, have to get the children ready for school, can't find your car keys, drive to work in heavy traffic, arrive late and can't find a parking space. Within the first two hours of an average day, six to twelve stressful events have already attacked you. You haven't had the time your body needs to restore equilibrium.

And the day is just beginning. What can you do?

You probably already have a good handle on what's causing your stress, the "stressors" in your life. You know them by name, most likely. But what about the catalysts and aggravators? They are just as important as the stressors. We'll get to know them as well because the key to controlling stress is learning how to modify your response, physically, emotionally and psychologically.

Then, you will learn how to create a daily coping plan for your individual needs and lifestyle. You can pick and choose what works for you and set up a 30-day trial. At the end of the month, you will have:

- identified and mastered the daily stresses in your life
- developed the tools and skills to handle the sudden and unexpected
- learned to put stress to work for you in a new and healthy way.

So, get ready to face your fears, find the facts, and take action to de-stress your stressful life!

Chapter 2

Where Does Stress Come from?

Before you even start reading, you can tell me where your stress comes from.

- ➢ Job
- ➢ Spouse
- ➢ Family
- ➢ House
- ➢ Car
- ➢ Traffic
- ➢ Shopping
- ➢ Organizations
- ➢ Friends
- ➢ Finances
- ➢ Health
- ➢ Aging
- ➢ Worry
- ➢ School
- ➢ All of the above

You may have crossed off a few things on this list or added other stressors. We all have a similar list. Most of these are external stresses, coming from our environment or lifestyle. You can also pick apart each one and narrow the stressor. For example, you might say, "My job is fine, but my boss is abusive, or I have to deal with a workload that isn't manageable tor three people, let alone one."

In addition to external stressors, there are catalysts which can contribute to the perception of stress and aggravators which intensify the response to stress. Catalysts exist within the person's internal, physical or emotional make-up, such as poor self-esteem, antagonism, chronic worry, compulsive addictive behaviors, and poor physical health. Aggravators are usually internal also, such as fears and phobias, illness, or any pathological responses to normal stress.

For example, my mother had a lifelong fear of birds stemming from an incident as a child in which a bird flew into her face and frightened her. Fear of birds became a stressor, and the aggravator was her memory of being attacked by one. Now, if I were afraid of birds because of my mother's experience, her story would be a catalyst causing me stress when I am around a bird.

Identifying the external stressors, and any catalysts or aggravators helps in the development of a daily stress-coping plan.

Take a few minutes to write down the stressors you recognize in these areas of your life: work, home, spouse and social. You can also use the list above if your prefer.

Chapter 3

Your Response to Stress

Stress takes a toll on body, mind and spirit. See if you recognize yourself in any of these symptoms.

The physical symptoms of stress include:
Headaches, colitis, insomnia, irritable bowel syndrome, chest pain, lack of energy, sweating, rapid pulse, heart palpitations, ulcers, fatigue, indigestion hypertension, irregular menstrual cycles, irregular pulse, flushing, sweating, and increased susceptibility to infection.

The emotional symptoms associated with stress include:
Irritability, worry, anxiety, anger, mood swings, apathy, depression, bitching, impatience, denial, and changes in dependency needs.

The psychological symptoms caused by stress are:

Memory loss, fears, withdrawal, inability to concentrate, panic attacks, crying jags, sleeplessness, addictions, compulsive behaviors, disillusionment, nightmares, eating disorders, loss of motivation, depression, phobias, disintegration of daily routines, forgetfulness, disorganization, and substance abuse.

Obviously all of the symptoms can be caused by a variety of illnesses and may have nothing to do with stress at any given time in your life. However, these are the types of symptoms that are rooted in the occurrence of the "fight-or-flight: syndrome that is usually produced by stress.

Here's what happens when you encounter a stressor: Begin with the neurons (nerve cells) of the hypothalamus, the part of the brain that connects the brain to the endocrine system and regulates your response to stress without any conscious thought or effort on your part.

The hypothalamus responds to a stressor by secreting a chemical that is transmitted by the neurons to the anterior pituitary gland which, in turn, begins to produce fifty different hormones, called corticosteroids. These include glucocorticoids which are involved in carbohydrate metabolism, mineralocorticoids such as aldosterone, and androgens.

Other chemical neurotransmitters, epinephrine and norepinephrine, are secreted to activate the Sympathetic Nervous System (SNS).

The Autonomic Nervous System (ANS) regulates your heart, vessels, and visceral smooth muscles. Epinephrine and norepinephrine increase the heart rate, cardiac output, blood pressure, release of liver glucose, production of hydrochloric acid in the stomach, and blood cholesterol levels. These hormones also cause constriction of peripheral blood vessels, and relaxation of bronchial air passages, decreased muscle tone and mobility in the bowels, relaxation of genito-urinary muscles, constriction of sphincters. What this all means is: when you are under stress, your heart is working harder and faster, your liver releases some of its stores of sugar into the blood stream to give you instant energy, your stomach increases the acid to allow you to digest food in the stomach more quickly, the bowels slow down to reserve whatever food is in them, the blood vessels in your legs contract to ready you for running away, your breathing passageways are readied to allow you to take deeper or more rapid breaths and your bowels and bladder stop working so that you don't have to stop to go to the bathroom when you should be fighting or fleeing.

In a split second, without you even realizing it, your brain has given your body its marching orders. "Fight or Flight."

Just as quickly and without fanfare, the Sympathetic Nervous System steps in to calm you down when the emergency ends. The SNS is responsible for relaxation, sleep, calmness, recovery, healing, growth, energy, immunity, control of emotions and maintenance of essential minerals.

Your heart needs to return to its normal, resting rate, lungs and breathing slow down, restoring the oxygen-carbon dioxide ratio, peripheral veins relax, muscle tone and mobility return to the bladder and bowels. Digestion in the gastro-intestinal system returns to normal and metabolism slows down.

While the physiological response to stress takes only seconds, recovery of equilibrium requires about thirty minutes. Time is needed for the emotional release, processing the event, physical rest, if possible, the return to normal and the restoration of equilibrium.

When there are too many stressors back to back, your body never has a chance to through the recovery cycle.

Chronic stress involves chemical and physiological changes, including depletion of thymus hormones which decreases your immunity to infections and disease; increase in the body metabolic rate placing demands on the pancreas to keep blood sugar stable; and, disturbance in the balance of amino acids production.

Chronic stress affects your heart. When cardiac output increases, the respiratory system responds by increasing the rate of respirations to increase the oxygen saturation in the blood and send extra oxygen to the muscle to prepare them for activity. The level of carbon dioxide goes down, producing a feeling of exhaustion, accompanied by cold feet and hands, dizziness, headache, fainting, panic attacks, yawning, sighing, anxiety, memory loss, and chest pain.

Your brain is not immune. Under chronic stress, neuro-chemical changes occur that can lead to mood swings, insomnia and depression.

Numerous studies have shown that chronic stress increases susceptibility to rhinoviruses that cause the common cold and upper respiratory infections. Research done by NASA showed the epinephrine and norepinephrine produce microscopic contraction band lesions in heart muscle. These fibers may damage the muscle without producing symptoms. This may explain why 50% of all heart attacks occur within forty-eight hours of a major life stress event.

Chronic stress also increases the depletion of thymus hormones which affects immunity; changes the body's metabolic rate placing demands on the pancreas to keep blood sugar stable; and, disturbs the balance of amino acids production.

Are you convinced yet that chronic stress is harmful to your body, mind and spirit?

List the physical, emotional and psychological symptoms you are regularly experiencing.

Chapter 4

Burned Out

One episode of unexpected, sudden stress may produce any of the symptoms mentioned in the last chapter. But more often, it is the thousand, minor, daily hassles of life, the chronic stressors that accumulate to generate overwhelming symptoms. Then, these accelerate the downward spiral toward burn-out.

Burn-out occurs when an ongoing confrontation with daily reality pits the human spirit against unchangeable situations day after day. No matter how hard you try, you cannot "fix" your work, your life, your family, or your problems. This ultimately leads to surrender, powerlessness, disillusionment, resignation, apathy, and exhaustion of caring energies.

The burned-out person feels stagnated in work, and often in personal life as well. You often feel inadequate, alone, empty, disillusioned, exhausted, unenthusiastic or ineffective. Caring becomes apathy, involvement produces distancing, openness turns into self-protectiveness, and trust drifts toward suspicion.

Burnout produces a recognizable progression of physical, psychological, emotional and spiritual symptoms.

There is the feeling that no matter how hard you try to change the situation, you cannot. You may not even have the energy to reverse the process. You feel powerless to make the changes necessary to return to a position of control.

In this environment, major life changes such as divorce, abandonment of relationships, and job loss frequently occur. Try to avoid making life-changing decisions if you are battling burn-out. You may regret leaving your job, your home or your marriage. Burn-out and depression go hand-in-hand. Both affect decision-making.

Preventive care in the form of stress reduction is the best approach to the treatment of burn-out. While you may recognize burn-out in the early stages, it may already be too late to reverse the course. Because the inner strength needed to battle burn-out is often lacking, you may need to seek outside, perhaps professional assistance, to stop the downward spiral.

Determine where you might be in the burn-out spiral.

Chapter 5

Coping

Developing a coping plan takes the commitment of time and energy, often at a time when you have neither. Sounds like you might even be adding more stress, however, these are simple steps you can try immediately while you prepare to establish a longer-term daily coping plan.

Learn to avoid, alter and accept.

Avoid battles not worth fighting. Pick and choose wisely which issues excite you, require extra time and energy, or endanger the rapport in a relationship. Think "hot-button" issues. While most of the time it's fine to feel passionate and become involved, not is not the time to invite this additional stress into your life. Let go of them for the moment.

Avoid perfectionism also. Perfectionism is unattainable, frustrating and neurotic. You can diagnose perfectionism by the presence of "should," "if only," and "ought" in your conversations, especially those with yourself. Unrealistic expectations of yourself are not healthy for you or your family. Let go of perfectionism for the moment.

Avoid comparisons. Perfectionism can also be rooted in comparing yourself to others. Tell yourself you don't have to be a "Super Mom," or like _____(fill in the blank). Let yourself be who you are meant to be, not the clone of someone else who probably has more problems and stress than you anyway. Don't bother trying to come up with excuses: "I just moved," "This is baby fat," "I've got five kids." You do not need excuses if you don't compare, and when you let go of perfectionism.

Avoid saying "yes" too much. No one be "all things to all people." Set limits on yourself and learn to say "No" when you need to. If you find it difficult to say "No," use other phrases, such as "I can't fit it into this week's schedule," "I'd love to be involved in that, but another time would be better," "You can't afford my services," "I'd like to help, but I will have to bring my 3-year-old along."

Phrases like these allow you to graciously decline, without using the word. "No." Learning to say "no" actually helps you to do more by doing less, but doing it better. Part of being in control of stress in your life also involves learning to say "no." Respect your time and energy as much as you respect others. For many people, *over-committed* translates into *overwhelmed*. Check your priorities to see if they line up with your commitments of time and energy.

Alter your attitude and self-talk. Don't tell me you are a pessimist by nature. That is a cop-out and a choice to look at life with a chip on your shoulder. Maintaining a sense of humor and developing a positive attitude are essential and attainable. Begin by learning to view the stress in your life as an enabler. It provides you with energy to finish a project, or the impetus to seek answers to a problem, or the power to champion a cause. You need a certain amount of stress just to get up and going each morning. By learning to work with it, you can harness it's energy in productive ways.

Alter your self-talk, all those words you hear in your head when no one else is around, or say to yourself. You remember the words you tell yourself far longer than those someone else tells you. Learn to exchange negative self-talk for positive.

For example:

I can't do it; I've never done it before.

Doing something new can be frightening, but also exciting. I don't have to do it perfectly the first time.

They're not here; they must have had an accident.

There's a logical reason for their lateness. It must be traffic.

I wish I were more attractive.

This outfit is great, but for someone else. I'll keep looking until I find what's right for me.

I'll never be able to handle all this work.

I can build on success. I can do this.

Alter your expectations of life. When my eldest son was about six he was a very pessimistic child. He was fussing about something when I told him to cross that bridge when he got to it.

He replied, "With my luck the bridge will be out and I'll fall into the lake and get my only pair of pants muddy."

I went to work to alter his perceptions and expectations of life. Today, as an adult he has one of the most positive outlooks on life of anyone I know.

Think about the qualities and characteristics others have told you they admire in you. Even if you don't see them yourself. Cultivate your strengths. Recognize your talents as well as your limitations. But give yourself extra credit for talents and strengths.

Accept what you cannot change. As you work on a coping plan, you may need to redefine your priorities and how best to deal with them on a daily basis.

Develop your respect for yourself, which must come before others will respect you. When you accept the stress in your life, you are disrespecting yourself, your time and energy. Controlling your stress is a sign of respect for yourself.

Respecting yourself requires that you learn to communicate your needs clearly and openly, using "I" statements, such as "I want," "I need," "I choose to." Begin today with some self-talk about your needs. When you have established what you want and need in your life, you will be able to set boundaries that lead to control of stress.

Accept the demands you place on yourself, but only it they are realistic. Demands are a source of strength, especially when they are realistic. When you accept others, yourself and situations as they truly are, not as you fear they might become, you can become more effective in dealing with them.

Remember: Serenity is not freedom from the storm, but peace within the storm.

Make a list of the ten accomplishments in your life that mean the most to you. Haven't taken a "sick day" in months? Give yourself credit for it. Are you a loyal friend who would drop everything to help out? List that. When you are finished, read your accomplishments daily.

Chapter 6

Change

The only person who likes change is a baby with a full diaper.

Change can be the source of a great deal of stress, along with physical and emotional symptoms, such as headaches, fatigue, insomnia, depression, indigestion, heart palpitations, increased susceptibility to illness and infection, colitis, fears, phobias, forgetfulness, dementia, nightmares, eating disorders, abuse and dependency disorders.

Change is like a beast threatening your status quo, your sense of security, and need for control.

But now that you know how to alter expectations and self-talk, take a new look at change. It may demand that you let go of the "security blankets" of past ways of doing things in order to embrace new challenges and opportunities for growth. We all have the illusion that we can manage change by controlling our environment, however, change can truly only be managed from within ourselves.

You have choices in life. You can cope with change, accept its inevitability, you can feel frustrated and stressed by change, or you can welcome the challenges, and take the reins of control over change.

Gandhi said, "You must be the change you wish to see in the world."

The first step in mastering change involves finding inner stability by better understanding yourself. How do you cope with change? Are you a person who rushes headlong into new experiences, or do you hang back, and let others take the first steps? Do you work best by creating a pros and cons list to evaluate the change?

Strive to develop an open mind and flexibility in the face of change. By relaxing your hold on the past, you can learn new ways. How much information do you need up-front? Or, can you learn as you go? What type of learner are you:

>   Do you prefer to have something explained verbally?
>   Do you prefer to read the manual or instructions?
>   Do you need hands-on experience to master something new?
>   Do you learn best by observing and copying an instructor's moves?

Change almost always involves learning new skills, new procedures, new policies, new methods of doing something, or just new ways of coping. When you have identified your learning type, you can approach change armed with the knowledge of how to structure the change to make it easier for you to control it.

Mastering change requires looking at life through new lenses, adjusting your frame of reference. Alexander Graham Bell wrote: "When one door closes, another door opens; but we often look so long and so regretfully upon the closed door that we do not see the ones which are open for us."

Look at the process of change as an adventure of discovery. Change is an unbroken horse, a challenge to control, but an opportunity to go to new places, to leave your comfort zone and to blaze new trails.

Change is really only a circumstance in need of improvement.

Try using problem-solving steps: identify the problem, brainstorm options, choose a solution, implement, and then, evaluate the solution. By focusing on this process, you may be able to breeze through the change without feeling overwhelmed by it.

To master change, you need knowledge, a plan, and sometimes, teamwork. Approach it with creative problem-solving. Learn to see problems as situations in need of correction or solutions. Your goals for mastering change then become finding ways to improve a situation, and programs or plans become the means by which your goals are achieved.

Whenever you are confronted by change, especially stressful change:

> Seek inner stability first.
> Try to open up to the experience with the calm of flexibility in the face of rigidity.

➢ Be willing to abandon any former (mis)perceptions and security blankets.
➢ Take the first step in a new direction.
➢ Take charge of the change and your stress.

A positive mindset helps. Try to look at change as an opportunity to be proactive, to anticipate the problems or challenges associated with change, to show resilience, and to define the vision for a pathway into the future. Change often requires more than "going with the flow." Learn to chart your own course.

Identify the changes in your present or near future that might produce stress, and begin to plan how you will control them.

Chapter 7

30 Days to De-Stress

Day 1

Create a space for yourself where you can relax, alone or with others.

Cultivate a pleasant environment by surrounding yourself with what you like whenever possible, whether it is flowers, houseplants, books, paintings or photos.

Keep in mind, however, that there is a line at which the things you enjoy become knickknacks that must be dusted frequently or plants that need watering and pruning. Don't add work for yourself in the name of beauty.

Look for small opportunities to improve your life. For example, make the laundry room the most delightful place in the house. Become aware of the demands your environment places on you and work to make changes to release you from the stress of these demands.

Bring beauty into your space. Investigate how color affects your moods and which colors make you happy. Paint a room a calming color, or if your space is very limited, try painting the inside of a closet or the back wall of a bookshelf. Once, I hung a door mirror on the back wall of a closet to brighten the space.

Color can brighten a mood, bring a smile to your face. Think about all of the ways you can bring pleasing color into your life. Your socks or the shoestrings of your athletic shoes. Paperclips on your desk. Dish towels in the kitchen. Eye make-up. File folders, sofa or bed pillows.

Make your space friendly and comfortable.

Give thought to lighting, temperature, noise, and smell. Perhaps you enjoy fragrant candles, a zen garden, or ocean sounds. Make it yours. Make it real. Make it relaxing.

Day 2

Take a stroll through an old photo album and enjoy your memories. My sisters and their daughters made a family memory book with old, as well as recent photos. How precious it is to see my great-grandmother in a photo on the same page as my grandchildren!

Don't have time or energy to create photo or memory albums? Collect some favorite photos and take them to a store that can make an album for you or send them to an online company to create a book.

Following vacation trips, I make a photo book at an online site and have easy and instant memories. The books are also great to share with visitors, much more pleasant to sitting through a show of all eight hundred of my photos from the trip.

Frame favorite photos and display them in your space. Don't be afraid to change them out as often as you wish. Think of other places to have photos at your fingertips, your cell phone, tablet or computer desktop, for example.

Day 3

Remind yourself that you are an enabler, not a magician. You cannot change anyone else's behavior. You can only change your own behavior and responses.

This is also a good time to limit your contact, if possible, with persons who thrive on drama in their lives or raise havoc in yours. Drama usually equates to high stress. You cannot fix their stress; you can only seek to control your own. So, if someone is bleeding their stress into your space, try to take a break from their presence, their story and their drama.

When that person is a spouse, child, parent, boss or co-worker, you might not be able to create that space. In that situation, separate the action from the actor. You can like/love someone without approving of or accepting what they are doing, or how they are living their lives.

Learning to set boundaries can help defuse some of the stress of dealing with people of drama. Do something each day that gives you energy, something that you live, something that please you.

Day 4

Vacation. We tend to think a week-long break from work or the daily routine is a vacation from stress. However, vacations are often stress-producers. Instead, try mini-vacays.

If you can find fifteen minutes during a day, or one hour a week, if daily isn't possible, make a date with yourself. Schedule a walk around the block, lunch in the park, a sunrise or sunset solo viewing party, a bubble bath without interruptions, a stroll through a favorite store, a cup of your favorite beverage, away from the demands of the day.

This isn't always possible, especially if you have young children. When you have little ones underfoot, use naptime for yourself and a good book, not for cleaning the kitchen or catching up with laundry. When they outgrow napping, institute an hour of "quiet play." Set aside special "quiet" toys that they can play with during that time so that they look forward to this time. Or, trade an hour with another mom. You watch hers one day and she watches yours another.

Do something that relaxes you, that involves a change of pace or scenery, during your mini-vacay.

Day 5

Take a deep breath and concentrate on a slow exhalation while tension melts from your limbs. Seriously, there's an art to this deep breathing business. You need to be seated comfortably first. Don't fret over where or how or if you should plant your feet or cross your legs in a yoga pose. Just sit down in your favorite chair. If you lie down, you might get so relaxed you'll go to sleep.

Close your eyes, or not, depending on what the toddler is up to.

Imagine a more peaceful place to be. Anywhere in the world. Where there are no clothes to be washed or dinner to be made or taxes to be filed.

Breathe in deeply through one or both nostrils. Pay no attention to the stuffiness on one side. Just breathe.

Count to whatever number pleases you, past five or six.

Then let the breath out with just as much deliberateness. Like you're blowing out birthday candles. You want to be quick enough to get all of them before someone has time to count them. But you have to control the breath to make it last for most of the imaginary flames.

Another version of slow breathing uses one of those mini-straws used for stirring coffee. Suck the air in through it, blow out around it. It's like resistance or weight-training for your lungs.

If you want to get fancy, try imagining all of the stress is dissipating with every breath. You are blowing it out with each lung-ful. Let stress ooze out of your pores, hairs, fingers and toes. Contract and relax a few muscles to enhance the imagery.

Or just breathe. Block out the traffic noise and the squealing toilet and the cat about to pounce on your lap.

Day 6

Have a massage. In Far Eastern medicine, massage is used to open blocked energy channels to improve your health. Massage relaxes tight muscles, reduces pain and improves circulation.

If you can't afford an hour, ask if the massage therapist can do a half-hour for half-price. Check out a massage school for a discount. If you are uncomfortable taking off clothing, try seeing a reflexologist for a foot massage.

Or, exchange massages with your spouse.

You don't need a fancy massage table or special oils. You can use baby oil, or olive oil with a drop of vanilla as a scent. Or move the massage to the shower and wash each other's backs.

Mani's and pedi's also fit into this stress-relieving day. Relax and enjoy a little pampering.

Day 7

Be a buddy to have a buddy. Stress often involves isolation. As stress mounts, you withdraw from relationships and activities that are normally beneficial. Seek support. Not answers, not advice, not solutions, just support.

A good friend won't need to know what's wrong, and won't offer unsolicited advice. Take a walk together; work on a jigsaw puzzle; bake something; discuss a book; take in a movie. Doing the normal things of life with someone who is accepting, uncritical and non-interfering can be restorative.

Give support to another and learn to accept it. Everyone feels helpless (and perhaps hopeless) at some time. Admit it and get on with it.

When someone needs you, be there for him or her. When you need someone, tell him or her. Find someone you can call or talk to any time. Someone you trust with your feelings.

Social media is a great way to develop a support system. But keep it private. Posting everything on Facebook is not the best plan. Once it's out there, you can't get it back and it will be there forever.

The best part of having a buddy is, you can have more than one. I have a group of four-to-six friends who have met weekly for lunch for more than a decade. And, I have an email support group of six. We exchange emails to encourage each other as we deal with similar demands and stresses in our lives.

To be successful with a buddy, always try to offer twice as much encouragement and support as you seek.

Day 8

Change your routine to refresh your life. Get up a few minutes earlier and go for a walk. Rearrange the furniture. Take a different route home from work. Wear your rings on different fingers. Order something new from a restaurant menu. Have dessert before your meal. Part your hair on the other side. Wear a new color you haven't worn before.

Getting into a rut can make life simpler, but also more boring. Sometimes making small changes that seem insignificant can create large differences in your well-being. Give it a try; change a habit today to change your life.

Day 9

Before you go to bed, think about your day. Focus on one good thing that happened each day.

Write it down.

A gratitude journal lets you keep track of the millions of little events which please, surprise and de-stress you every day. Even when you have had a miserable day, the habit of looking for one positive thing, no matter how trivial, will help you to re-frame the difficult days.

An attitude of gratitude pervades your world with a positive spirit.

Day 10

Learn to recognize the difference between a stress-producing complaint and constructive criticism. Think about this for a moment. Someone criticizes you, or something you have done. Do you internalize their words? Does criticism diminish your self-worth? Do you respond offensively with a criticism of your own? When this type of situation escalates, stress grows by leaps and bounds.

Try first to reframe criticism. Imagine the person really has your best interests at heart. Their words are true, spoken in love, for your benefit. It's usually hard to think this way. Criticism stings. You tend to confuse the action with the actor. You take their words personally.

Step back from the hurt. And try to keep from being instantly defensive.

Can you determine what prompted the criticism? If not, ask for clarification by repeating the person's words followed by a question. "What I hear you say is… Have I gotten it correctly."

It's not that you want to hear the criticism twice, but if the person wasn't clear, he'll have the opportunity to rephrase. And the pause gives you the chance to develop a response that is less defensive.

When criticism is constructive, it's aimed at your behavior, not your person. The words describe a behavior that you have the power and ability to correct. But you must decide if you want to change that behavior. Remember: you do not have control over the behavior of the person complaining. You do have control over your behavior.

Sometimes it is appropriate to ask for suggestions to help you make the changes; other times, it's better to simply say, "I'll work on that." And then seek your own solutions.

If you make changes, edit your own self-talk. Don't let criticism echo in your mind or become a regular part of your inner monologue. Remind yourself that you are no longer that person.

Many years ago, someone told me that I wasn't a team player. I took the criticism and tried very hard to figure out what it meant and how to change that perception. Today, no one could say that to me, and I need to stop saying it to myself. Along with the words my parents said about living up to my potential.

Counter criticism with positive self-talk. "I play nicely with others," is a good place to start.

By dealing with constructive criticism with an open and flexible mind, you can grow as a person, improve relationships with others, and decrease the interpersonal friction that causes stress.

Day 11

Try a new food. Or a new restaurant. Have dessert before your meal. There are really no rules in a restaurant that require you to order a meal in a certain way. Unless you are eating at a very expensive, exclusive place that induces stress the minute you walk in.

Eating out, even in a party of two, can be a stressful or a stress-reducing event. Sometimes it helps to decide in advance what you want to eat. If you are trying to control your diet, that's generally a good idea. But leave room for surprise, for novelty, for flexibility.

Have an appetizer for the main course. Or order three side dishes. You'll often cut the calories and the cost, and still have plenty of food.

If you really want to change things up when you're eating out, try a progressive dinner. Go to one restaurant for an appetizer, another for salad or soup, a third for the main dish and stop for ice cream on the way home.

Why go to all this fuss? Deciding where and what to eat can be stressful. Giving yourself permission to have fun, to try something new or different, can reduce stress.

Day 12

Laugh. Laughter releases endorphins, chemicals in your brain that restore calm.

Remember the hypothalamus and its role in stress? It is also active in combating stress. During exercise, excitement, pain, food consumption, laughing and making love, the hypothalamus and the pituitary gland release endorphins which can give you a "runner's high," a feeling of calm, joy, pain relief, and well-being.

Research has shown that laughter helps your heart by decreasing high blood pressure, and increasing blood vessel elasticity and flow.

Laughter relieves muscle tension and pain for up to forty-five minutes. Endorphins resemble the chemical make-up of opioid pain medications, and are called "Nature's pain medicine."

The stress hormones cortisol and adrenaline are reduced when people laugh. And laughter improves your immunity to infection and diseases.

You know what tickles your funny bone. Whether it's television comedy or a funny movie, comic strips, or play, indulge to laugh off stress. Have fun.

Day 13

If you socialize with co-workers, keep it social, not a rehash of the day's tensions. Avoid shop talk outside of work. Try not to bring it home with you and let work stress take over your leisure time.

This doesn't mean you can't discuss with your spouse something from your job that's bothering you. But before you start, establish whether you want advice, sympathy, solutions or a friendly ear. This is especially important if you are sharing with a problem-solver personality.

Problem-solvers engage in self-talk while listening. They cannot wait to jump in with suggestions. "Have you tried …?" When you don't want solutions, say so first to help the listener focus on your words rather than answers to your problems.

When you do want suggestions to your problems, ask for them, but set limits. Most people can only deal with one or two solutions or changes at one time. Stop your listener after the first two suggestions. Be sure also to give yourself permission to reject someone else's ideas of how to handle your issues. You are responsible for your behavior and for your problems.

Using some deep breathing techniques in the car as you drive home can help you avoid bringing home stress.

Once you master leaving work stress at work, you will notice how much more restful weekends and vacations are.

Day 14

Have a diet check-up. Eating too much fast food, deep fried, sugar-laden foods? What about your caffeine intake?

What you eat can affect how you deal with stress. Some foods, such as those with high levels of salt, sugar and fats, lessen your ability to handle stress. Sodas, beverages with caffeine or alcohol increase stress.

High-fiber foods, raw fruits and vegetables help to fight high cholesterol, and blood pressure, and stress. Fiber foods include: whole grains and heart-healthy nuts. Whole grain foods offer vitamin E, potassium, and pantothenic acid, one of the stress-fighting B vitamins. Nuts are high in magnesium. Good choices include: oatmeal, bran cereal, unsalted almonds, cashews, sunflower and pumpkin seeds.

The B vitamins are well known for relieving stress and depression. You can find them in breads, and some vegetables.

Choose fruits and veggies high in potassium and low in sodium, such as bananas, sweet potatoes and oranges. Select those with vitamins A and D, and folic acid to improve your overall general health. Good choices are: dark green, leafy vegetables.

Drink more water. Staying well-hydrated helps every system of the body to work more efficiently. Water helps skin, bowels, and kidneys. Drinking six to eight glasses of water also encourages weight loss. Try keeping water close at hand to remind you to drink it more frequently. To improve the flavor and add variety, you can freeze pieces of fresh fruit or mint leaves in ice cubes to add to your glass of water.

The old adage, "you are what you eat," is definitely true when it comes to managing stress. Balance your diet, balance your life.

Day 15

Make rest a part of the daily plan. Try to set aside 15 minutes every day for relaxation or doing something you enjoy. There's no such thing as catching up with sleep on the weekend.

Adequate sleep, at least seven hours per night aids stress management, memory, ability to concentrate and learn, weight loss, mood, heart health and immune function. Sleep deprivation can cause falls, mistakes and auto accidents.

Some ideas for relaxation: Take a warm bath. Get involved in your favorite hobby or learn a new hobby. Take ten-fifteen minutes to sit quietly and breathe deeply. Start an exercise program. Take a short nap. Find a comfortable place for light reading

Most importantly, too little sleep leaves you too tired to enjoy life. So, take a fifteen minute break to relax, breathe deeply and drink a glass of water. Leave the digital devices in another room, experts suggest disconnecting an hour before bedtime. And get your seven to nine hours of shut-eye tonight.

Day 16

Simplify your life. You probably cannot accomplish this in one day, but you can start the journey. Consider time and treasure: what can you do without? How can you de-clutter your calendar and your environment so that you can save time and money and stress?

Begin by prioritizing what's most important to you and eliminating the trivial. Simplify your day by creating a "To Do" list, or two: one for today and one for a day when you have extra time and infrequently-done tasks.

Learn simpler ways to accomplish daily tasks at work and at home to save time and energy. Eliminate time-wasters such as junk mail and junk phone calls. Using an egg timer helps you control callers who go on and on. Set it when you answer the call and when it goes off, tell the caller you have to go now.

Simplify your closets and dresser drawers on a day when you have time for one of those infrequently-done tasks, or set aside a day for "spring cleaning." Donate what you don't need.

Allow your life to proceed at a slightly slower pace. If you get up fifteen minutes earlier, you won't have to rush to get ready in the morning. If you practice being a few minutes early for appointments, you won't stress over the traffic on the way there. If you drive a little more slowly, you will save gas and money and be safe.

Organizing your stuff, your time and your life gives you a sense of control, instead of chaos.

Day 17

Make exercise a part of your daily life. Try to increase the number of steps you take each day. If you have a pedometer and want to keep track, begin with trying to get three thousand steps a day and work your way up to ten thousand. Park a little farther from the door of the store, or your job. Take the stairs instead of the elevator, or take a walk during lunch or after dinner.

The easiest way to get more exercise is to leave the remote on top of the television, and get up to change channels.

Join an exercise or yoga class. Recruit a buddy to go along and you will be more likely to stick with it. Exercise or enjoy sports with your children or walk your dog and you will all benefit.

Invest in hand weights or use a bottle of water or can of food for resistance exercises. Skip rope, ride a bike, skate, swim. Make a fun activity part of your daily life.

Remember, exercise also releases endorphins in your brain for a calming effect, sometimes called a "runner's high."

Day 18

Choose not to waste time on guilt, regret or worry about the past. Events exist in time, but feelings do not. The event may be past, but the feelings can linger on. Let go of both. Stop trying to control the past. Make peace.

Watch out for high expectations of yourself that can stress and depress you. Ask yourself where these expectations come from. Are you comparing yourself to someone else? You cannot excel at who you are until you walk away from comparing yourself to others. Work at living up to your own self-defined potential, not someone else' expectations of you.

Learn to let go of perfectionism.

Look for new ways to cope. Sometimes making small changes in other areas of your life helps to make changes in the unchangeable. When situations are the most unchangeable, stop trying to control them. Let go of doing what you have done in the past, especially if it obviously isn't working. Learn to accept what you cannot change instead of feeling constantly frustrated.

Day 19

Enjoy nature. Studies have shown that surgical patients use less pain medication and recover more quickly when they have a view of trees, rather than the building next door.

Get out of the house, take a walk, visit a garden, or grow one yourself. But be careful not to equate relating to nature with getting a pet, a plant or a garden if the time and energy demands of taking care of a living thing adds to your stress. And watch out for those times of the year when allergies, or weather make being outdoors a problem for you.

Look up. Studying the sky and clouds can be wonderfully relaxing.

Easy ways to get closer to nature: create a cactus garden in a pot. Cacti are usually slow-growers with less need for water. Even better, a flat bowl of sand and a small rake for a Japanese zen garden. Want a pet? Think about a fish tank. The sounds and sights of fish in an aquarium can be relaxing, and fish don't have to be taken outside every few hours.

Day 20

Nurture someone else. Being in love, enjoying romantic attraction, or nurturing a baby all release the hormone oxytocin from the pituitary gland in the brain. Oxytocin controls fear, anxiety and stress, and gives you a sense of well-being and calm.

This hormone also enhances social interactions. So, it's really a cart-and-horse situation: fall in love, your pituitary release oxytocin which helps you relax and enjoy each other, which produces more oxytocin.

Isn't love wonderful?

Day 21

Respect yourself. Talk positively about and to yourself. Accept yourself. Choose your attitude.

Be aware of your emotions. Admit your feelings, even if only to yourself. Some people find keeping a written journal of emotions helpful.

Own your feelings. They are yours, and it's okay to feel as you do. Where you get into trouble is allowing feelings to control actions. Investigate your feelings. Are they based on reality? Is there some aspect of a situation or environment that you can change to lessen negative feelings or enhance positive ones?

Accept responsibility for your feelings, and your behavior in response to your feelings.

Match what you are experiencing to what you are saying. A discrepancy between what you say and feel brings confusion, especially to relationships, often causing a breakdown in communications.

Integrate your emotions, intellect and will to grow as a person. You can choose to focus on anger, bitterness, frustration, depression and stress. Or, you can try to put these negative emotions aside, learn to cope, and get on with life.

Finally, learn when to surrender. But consider a new definition for "surrender." Don't think of it as "giving up" or "giving in," but rather as a battle for yourself. In the end, you win. Surrender does not compromise who you are, but helps you become who you are supposed to be.

Day 22

Practice doing one thing at a time. Focus on it, do it more slowly and intentionally. Do what you're doing more slowly, more intentionally, with greater awareness and respect. Multi-tasking often gives a false sense of managing time.

Prioritize activities. Do what's most important first whenever you can so that you don't end up living under the tyranny of the urgent. Controlling the priorities in your daily life let's you control the stress as well.

Remember, it takes less energy to get an unpleasant task done right now, rather than worry about it all day.

Delegate, delegate, delegate. You do not have to be "all things to all people." Give away the jobs, chores, tasks that someone else can perform. Consider your children: by teaching them how to perform daily chores, giving them responsibility, you are preparing them for their futures. Yes, you will need to supervise them. Yes, they will make mistakes. But in the end, you are doing them a favor by enlisting their help with household chores and daily tasks.

Learn to let go.

Day 23

Set goals for yourself. Goals are like New Year's Resolutions that make sense, are easier and more rewarding to keep, and help you see where you're headed. Goals give you direction and benchmarks.

The easiest way to make goals is to consider where you want to be one year and five years from now. Think about the various areas of your life: health and wellness, social, work, family, education, religion. Want to lose weight, read a certain number of books, strengthen relationships, volunteer in your community, complete your education, achieve an accomplishment at work? These are all either short-term or long-range goals.

Write down your goals.

Next, consider what you need to do to achieve your goals. Those action steps will give you direction toward achieving your goals. Because I use goals as my New Year's resolutions, the time frame is built in. I plan to complete these goals within a calendar year. At the end of March, if I haven't made some progress on each one, I know I'd better get moving, or delete that goal.

Day 24

Use prayer, meditation, or yoga to relieve stress. Take your choice; they all help you relax and de-stress. You will need fifteen to thirty minutes, and a quiet spot. For yoga, you might also want instruction in a class or book or video. Prayer or meditation don't require any special techniques, just freedom from distractions.

Sit or walk, keep eyes open or closed, whatever you are comfortable with. If you don't know how to get started, try reading the Bible, or an inspirational book for a few minutes. Then close the book and think about what you have read. How does it apply to your life, what lessons can you learn from it?

Don't worry if your mind wanders, just bring your focus back when you realize you've gone astray. Prayer is simply talking to God, aloud, or silently, or in writing. You don't need to use formal "church" language. Be yourself (and let Him be Himself). Begin by thanking God for the day, for this few minutes of solitude. You can talk to Him like He's an old friend catching up on your latest.

Allow time to listen. Quiet time. Stress-free moments , Stretch. Take a deep breath. Focus on your breathing. On your heartbeat. On the air around you. On your senses: what you see, smell, hear, touch. Listen to your heart to give you direction.

Some call this "mindfulness," being present in the moment. When you are present in the moment, there's no room for the regrets, guilt or pain of the past or for the worry for the future.

Day 25

Time your activities according to your biorhythms. Most people know if they are early birds or night owls. If you are a morning person, schedule your most difficult or time-consuming tasks in the morning, as much as possible. When you are at your peak energy and focus, it will be easier to breeze through the job. If your peak for productivity is later in the day, use that to your advantage.

In addition to a daily biorhythm, we also have annual ones. What month of the year do you feel draggy, tend toward illnesses, or become depressed? Do you struggle with certain holidays or other dates? Those times of the year you are more vulnerable to ordinary stresses, and they also add their own difficulties.

But once you have identified the times that feel challenging year after year, you can plan for them so they don't sneak up on you and lay you low. Scientists have found the winter months to be problematic for some people who live in the northern regions with very little sunlight. February was the month that got me down. I began to use that time to plan a vacation and discovered that the anticipation of summer helped me to get through a dreary month.

If you notice a specific time during the year depresses you, be sure to check your nutrition during that time. It's easy to fall into bad habits when you are under stress, and certain holidays encourage the intake of too much sugar, and alcohol. Plan ahead in anticipation of these times.

Day 26

Face fears. Remember the "fight or flight" syndrome? It produces a physical response which can sometimes be inappropriate for the stressor. Fear is a response to a perceived threat or event which may or may not be a real threat.

It would be normal, and even healthy, to be afraid if you hear footsteps behind you as you walk alone in an alley after dark. Your fight or flight reaction engages appropriately to prepare you to confront or flee from the cause of your fear. On the other hand, it might not be normal or healthy for an adult to be afraid of a monster under your bed. If your flight or flight responses arises every night when you go to bed, you may need to determine the source of your fear and deal with it.

When your fears are irrational, seek the facts. Armed with the facts, you may be able to lay the fear to rest. Fear is an emotion, and emotions do not exist in a vacuum. They always co-exist with behaviors. Modify your behavior, and you can often handle your fears.

You've heard the advice, "Fake it until you make it." Take action to fight your fears, first by telling yourself you can beat them. Then, learn how and make a plan.

Day 27

Bake. Cookies, cupcakes, bread. Carbohydrate foods contain the B vitamins that fight depression and stress. But the act of creation, the smell of foods and the sight of these goodies also bring a sense of satisfaction.

Baking bread is especially helpful in combating stress because one of the early steps in the process is kneading. The physical effort of kneading bread can help you release stress, as well as other negative emotions. Find a simple whole wheat recipe, invest in a couple loaf pans and give bread-baking a try.

The product of your labors will amaze and delight you.

Day 28

Approach relationships with respect for the other person. Focus your attention on the other person, the words your hear, the unspoken, the body language. Ask questions to clarify your understanding. The meaning of words can change depending on experiences, roles, education, emotions, expectations, and background noise.

Think about your feelings. Leave the past in the past. Deal in the present.

Suspend your inner voice, blame, criticism, problem-solving. Just listen. Use small talk to smooth over differences. Does it really matter if you don't solve the pressing problems of the world? Sometimes just being together, sitting side-by-side, watching the day go by are all you need to do.

Touch, hug, put an arm around someone's shoulder, if appropriate. Work or play together. Make plans for time together. Invest in your todays for pay-off tomorrow. Be positive and gentle with each other. Learn to negotiate and be flexible.

Listen. To others as well as to yourself.

Day 29

Seek joy. Andrew Carnegie advised, "If you want to be happy, set a goal that commands your thoughts, liberates your energy, and inspires your hopes."

Never postpone joy. Make it your conscious choice today and every day. When you actively seek joy, there's less room in your life for stress or other negative emotions.

Begin by asking yourself what makes you happy. Use the journalists' "W" questions: Who? What? Where? When? And Why? Identify what brings a smile to your face and contentment to your heart.

If you can find nothing in your life that brings joy, as a friend what works for them, try it, or do the opposite. Then fake joy until you feel it. Smile. Share the smile with someone as if the two of you have some secret no one else knows.

Practice sharing a smile over the telephone. Ask if the person can hear a smile in your voice. If the answer is negative, work on your voice, tone or words until the joy comes through. When another person can sense your joy, you will also.

Day 30

The keys to a happy life are: something to do, someone to love, something to look forward to.

When what you do brings more stress than joy into your life, it may be time to make some changes. Sometimes you are trapped by the circumstances of life: an unfulfilling job, a family to support, poor health, bills to pay. You cannot change what you do.

When situations are the most unchangeable, let go of trying to control them. Stop doing what you have done in the past, which obviously isn't working. Look for new ways to cope. You might be able to make "local" instead of "global" changes, small adjustment that will ease the stress of the unchangeable.

When circumstances are unchangeable, remember that stress has two parts: the stressor and your response. If you cannot modify the stressor, examine what you can do about your response. There are things you cannot change. Yourself, your behavior, your stress responses are not among them.

Let go. Learn to say "No." Choose your words, replacing "I should," with "I choose," and "I can't" with "I won't."

Doing less, but doing it better might be more realistic for you, at this time. You can always resume or add new activities as you begin to feel better. Although it may be difficult for you to accept, you cannot be "all things to all people." Let yourself off the hook as you re-define who you are and what you want to do.

Someone to love. You live alone. Have no family, friends, pet. Get out of the house. Go to the library. Talk to the librarian. Volunteer to read a book to a child. Go to a school. Check into becoming a tutor to a child with reading problems. Go to a college. Ask about students who live to far from home to go there for the holidays. Chances are, they come from a foreign country and would love to learn about your holiday traditions. Go to a church. They all welcome strangers. Volunteer at the zoo or the animal shelter. Someone there needs your attention.

Stay home and call someone you haven't talked to in years. Meet your neighbors. You don't have to bake cookies to take to them, although that's welcomed in most households. Pick up a Starbucks gift card and offer to share it with someone.

Something to look forward to comes from setting goals for yourself. Make time on a regular basis to listen to your heart, examine your priorities, and re-order your life goals. Make a "bucket list." Then make a plan to accomplish the items on that list.

Chapter 8

Welcome to your Stress-Free Life!

This book is a self-help recovery program for stress-sufferers.

By recognizing the symptoms, the earlier the better, and beginning a plan to decrease stress in your life, you can take ownership of your life, your happiness, and your stress.

Welcome to the never-ending journey—one that can be exciting, fulfilling and fun, with some stress that keeps you on your toes. By using these techniques to de-stress your days, you can restore your life to enjoy what you do, whom you love and what you are looking forward to.

About the Author

Joyce Good Henderson always knew she could "write the book on stress" if she had had the time when she was a single mom to five children. But now that the children are grown and married with kids of their own, she's learned that stress doesn't magically disappear, it just takes on new forms.

The author has thirteen published books, works as a homecare nurse, teaches wellness classes to seniors, coaches other writers, leads medical mission teams with her husband to Ecuador, grows vegetables in her backyard, has thirteen grandchildren (and still counting), and never met a stressor she didn't latch onto. She hopes the information and suggestions in this book help you as much as they've helped her.

You can find her other nonfiction books and novels at www.Amazon.com.